Echoes Of Me

Poems of Loss, Love, and Healing.

By

Rachel Norman

R&R Publishing

Echoes of Me: Poems of Loss and Healing
© 2025 Rachel Norman

This is a work of creative nonfiction. Names, characters, and incidents are drawn from the author's personal experiences and imagination. Any resemblance to actual persons, living or dead, is purely coincidental unless otherwise stated.

Published by:
Randrnorman Publishing LLC
Flat Rock, Mi

ISBN: 979-8-218-79908-3
Library of Congress Control Number: [Optional, if you obtain one]

Cover Design: Rachel Norman
Book Design: Randrnorman Publishing LLC

Printed in the United States of America

Dedication

I dedicate this book to all the people God placed in my life to teach me lessons and give me strength. God's hand has always been upon me, even when I could not see it—and for that, I am deeply thankful.

I also dedicate this book to my dad. Thank you for loving me even when I made it difficult. I'm sorry for being a tough teen, and I'm grateful for your unwavering love.

Acknowledgments

First and foremost, I give all glory and thanks to God—my Redeemer, my Refuge, and the One who never stopped pursuing me. Without His grace, none of these words would have been written, and I would still be lost in the shadows. Thank You, Lord, for healing the broken pieces and giving me a voice to speak through the pain.

To my family—thank you for walking with me, even when the road was unclear. Your love and presence, even in silence, have been felt deeply.

To the people who caused me pain: I turned that pain into purpose. These poems are proof that God can take what was meant to harm me and use it for healing.

To my younger self: I see you. I honor you. You survived, and I'm proud of you for picking up the pen instead of giving up.

And to every reader holding this book: thank you. Thank you for listening to my echoes. If you see yourself in these pages, may you know you're not alone—and may you never forget that healing is possible, and your story still matters.

With all my heart,
Rachel Norman

Preface

Echoes of Me is a reflection of my voice across different seasons—some when I was lost, and others when I was found again in Christ. These poems were not written for an audience, at least not at first. They were written to survive. To breathe. To give language to what I couldn't always say out loud.

Some of these words came from the struggle between living and merely surviving. I made choices during that time—some wild, some out of character. I walked away from God and from everyone in my life. I tried doing life my own way, and in the process, I hurt a lot of people. These poems reflect what I was feeling and seeing in those moments. While some are more positive than others, there's a deep undercurrent of pain and negativity that I may not have fully expressed in each piece, but that lived beneath every line.

These poems are my lifetime's work—the ones I chose to keep while discarding so many more.

Many of these pieces began in my teen years, when I was desperately searching for belonging, wrestling with identity, and facing grief and trauma far too early. Others were written later, after I returned to God and began the slow, sacred work of healing—letting Him piece back together the broken fragments of my life.

This book is raw. It's messy. It's a mixture of pain, hope, anger, love, confusion, and faith. But most of all, it's honest. These are my echoes -words that still reverberate in my soul, shaping me into the woman I'm still becoming.

I hope you find pieces of yourself in these pages. I hope you feel seen, understood, and reminded that no matter how far we fall, there is a God who still calls us back to Him. And in that call, we rediscover not only His love—but our voice.

— Rachel Norman

Foreword

Echoes of Me is more than a collection of poems—it is a testimony. These words carry the weight of my past, the wrestle of my pain, and the beauty of my redemption. Some of these pieces were written in the silence of my teenage struggles, when I didn't know how to pray, only how to bleed through a pen. Others were born from my return to God, when His grace became louder than my shame and His love rewrote the chapters I thought were finished.

This book is a journey—from brokenness to becoming, from wandering to worship, from questioning to trusting again. Every poem is a piece of who I was, who I became, and who I am still becoming through God's mercy.

I didn't write this for perfection—I wrote it for the girls who thought they'd never find healing, for the mothers still carrying childhood wounds, for the survivors learning to breathe again, and for anyone who has ever whispered, "God, where are You?"

My prayer is that within these pages, you hear your own echoes—your own cries, hopes, and healing. And more than anything, I pray you hear the whisper of a God who never left your side.

Rachel Norman
Author of *Echoes of Me*

Table of Contents

Preface II

Foreword III

Introduction..X

Part One..1

Echoes of Me..2

I'm a Writer..4

Perspective 5

Cult 6

Words 7

In Between the Lines 8

Foster Kid 9

Childhood Friends 10

I Have Lost Myself 12

Questions...14

I'm Struggling 15

Death Destroys..16

I'm Worthy..18

My Story..20

Lost identity...22

Canceled 23

I'm Lost..24

Fighting *26*

Death *27*

Unlovable One *28*

It's Terminal.. *30*

Anger... *32*

Growing Up *33*

I Don't Belong *34*

Letting Go *36*

Dreaming *37*

The Motherless Daughter *38*

God, Where Are You? *39*

Cloud of Grief.. *40*

Fragile *41*

Look into My Eyes!... *42*

What Is Love? *44*

Back to Me *46*

Survivor *48*

I Don't Know What to Say *49*

Let's Talk... *50*

I Will Overcome *51*

No More... *52*

Dreamer *53*

Streets 54

Teen Years 55

Neglect 56

Tribe 58

God's Angels 59

Mother 60

Children 62

Goodbye mother 64

The Fire Inside 66

Anger Within 68

Memories of You 70

Still, I Stayed 72

Left With Nothing but Silence 74

Vulnerable 75

Becoming a Woman 76

I Surrendered to God 77

Ride or die 78

Boy to a Man 84

Baby Girl 86

Growing Into Me 88

Remember When! 90

Grow 92

God's Grace 94

Life Cycle 96

Life Should Be Lived.. 97

Learning 98

Father... 99

Life Is Not What It Seems 100

The bond between Mother and Daughter.................. 101

The Unborn Child 102

Angel of Mine 103

Goodbye Sister 104

Let It Go! 106

Parenting 107

My dearest son 108

My dearest daughter 110

Growing Old 112

Cancer 114

Scars... 115

Daily Mantra 116

Thank You! 118

About the Author.. 120

Other Books by Rachel Norman 122

Introduction

Echoes of Me is more than a collection of poems—it's a journal of my soul. These words weren't written for applause. They were written for survival. They were scratched out in moments when I couldn't speak my truth out loud—when the pain, confusion, or silence was too heavy to carry any other way. This book holds pieces of my past, some from seasons I never thought I'd make it through.

Some of these pieces were written in the shadows of my teenage years, when pain echoed louder than purpose. When the world felt too sharp and I didn't know how to soften it. I was trying to find myself in the middle of chaos, trying to navigate loss, trauma, and identity while pretending I had it all together. Poetry became my outlet— my hiding place and my safe release. These early writings reflect a heart searching for answers in a world that gave few.

But most of the words you'll read here were written after I found my way back to God—after I stopped running, after I realized that healing could still happen, even after everything. These poems were birthed in the quiet spaces of rebuilding, when grace began to stitch the broken places back together, when I was learning, slowly, to believe again—in love, in redemption, and in myself.

This book is a reflection of both the wandering and the returning. It holds grief and growth, anger and redemption, questions and prayers. It's a story of leaving and of coming home again—not just to God, but to the truest version of me. Every piece is a snapshot of a moment I survived or a thought that shaped me. Some are hard to read even now. Others make me smile with gratitude. All of them are real.

If you've ever felt lost, unworthy, forgotten, or on the edge of giving up—I hope these pages whisper back to you, "You're not alone." I hope they remind you that your story isn't over. That even in the silence, God is still writing. That there is beauty in brokenness and power in being honest about where you've been.

These poems aren't perfect. But they're mine. And they're for anyone who has ever needed a reminder that healing is possible. That light can reach even the darkest places. That faith can be rebuilt, and that no matter how far you've gone, God is still calling you home.

Welcome to the echoes of me.

— Rachel

Part One
Echoes of Me

Echoes of Me

You hear a voice, soft but raw—
a whisper rising from broken places.
It's me.
The version of myself I buried
beneath shame, grief, and silence.

Every tear I never cried aloud
is etched in these lines.
Every scream I swallowed
is a stanza I survived.
These are not just words—
they're echoes
of who I used to be.

The girl who prayed through pain
but doubted she was heard.
The woman who walked away from God
then limped her way back—
bleeding, but breathing.
Torn, but trying.

You'll hear echoes of love
and echoes of loss,
the ache of abandonment
and the fragile hope that healed it.
These poems are pieces of me—

not polished, not perfect,
but proof that I'm still standing.

So, if you're searching
for your own reflection
in a world that doesn't see you—
sit with me in these pages.
Listen closely.
And maybe you'll hear
echoes of you, too.

— Rachel Norman

I'm a Writer

I write out my heart.
I put these words down so I may release them from me
just like when I say the words, I may release them into the world.

I write out my heart.
I write out my pain.
I write out everything.

So, I may release them from me.
I write it out so I may process this feeling and not hold it in.
I write it so I may believe it once again.

Have you ever lost everything—even your soul?
Nowhere to go, nowhere to run.
I write it out so I won't lose my soul again.
I write it out so I can let it go.
I write it, so my soul can grow.

I write out the compassion or passion that lingers inside of me.
I write these words, so you know you are not alone.

I am a writer with a story to tell.

Perspective

You say you are right.
They say you are wrong.
It is all in the perspective—
and how it is seen.

Do we fight and stand up
for what we believe is right?
Or do we just go along
with what they tell us to believe?

It is all in the perspective—
and how it is seen.

Life is full of mystery,
and yet we don't want to discover it.
We want to live—
and just be.

It is in the perspective—
and how it is seen.

Are we free?
Or are we just living
how they want us to be?

Life should be carefree,
but we are always fighting—
you and me.

It is in the perspective—
and how it is seen.

What do you see?

Cult

You taught me about trust issues,

as you washed my brain of what true love was.
You brought me up in a world of lies
that only furthered my anxiety.
You made me believe it was me
because I would not comply.
You made me want to hide from all religion
and not believe God was real.
You killed all my dreams
and told me I needed to be content in life.
I learned all your tricks
and applied them to the next guy.
When I walked away,
you left me alone and shunned me
from the only world I had ever known.
You told me I couldn't be lovable.
You made me feel like it was me—
I was the problem.
I wasn't allowed to question or grow.
I had to stay inside your box.
You labeled me a troublemaker or an attention seeker
because I just wanted to know.
Cult is what I learned you are, and I had to let you go.

Words

The words you say can build people up or tear them down.
Watch what you say.
They can cause fear when no one is around, or they can bring dreams into reality.

Words have the power to change a person's life.
The words can cut like a knife, or they can empower you.
What do you choose to say?

Words can bring things to life or cause someone pain.
Watch what you say,
or you may be the one causing someone else a stain on their heart.

Words can bring people together or tear them apart.
Watch what you say.
Be the light in this world instead and use your words to build up people's life's.

In Between the Lines

I read in between the lines.
I am an observer, and I watch everyone.
I read all the books, but I know they are not what
they seem.
I read in between the lines and see what you
really mean.

I am the observer, and I know you cannot be
honest with me.
It's okay, and it's alright—you owe me nothing,
and I will keep my distance from you.

I am an observer, and I know how hard it is for
you
to be truthful with me.

Lies are all you know,
and I will not be caught up in your deceit.

I read in between the lines,
and I know what you really mean.

Foster Kid

They took me from my home today—
said it wasn't safe to stay.
Told my parents, *"Get them out of Detroit,
or you'll never see your kids again."*

Now I'm somewhere unfamiliar,
with strangers calling the shots,
in a house that's not a home,
sleeping in a bed that isn't mine.

I am a foster kid.
Taught to follow rules I never made,
expected to smile through the pain,
to survive—but never really live.

They took my rights, my roots, my voice.
They left a scar they'll never see.

I am a foster kid—
and though I didn't choose this life,
I'm still here,
trying to hold on to hope,
one day at a time.

Childhood Friends

My childhood friends taught me to love.
They taught me how to be loyal and forgive.
My childhood friends taught me who I am.
They told me their stories and made me see the
world through their eyes.

My childhood friends taught me life is so full of
joy, no matter the pain.
My heart is forever stained with their memories
of us growing up together.
We said we would never be apart, but we
quickly learned we had our parts in each other's
lives.

My childhood friends, may your life hold
everything you ever wanted.
Thank you for being my childhood friends.

For my mother
The one who gave me life and shaped my soul.
Your love is still the loudest echo in me.

I Have Lost Myself

I have lost myself in a world so demanding.
The world has made me feel as though I'm standing alone,
in a world full of people.

I was made not to fit in or stand out.
I was made to be extraordinary
when all I wanted was to be ordinary.
I was made to believe I don't matter,
and that I have no gifts to give.

I'm me… but who am I?

I am a child of God who has survived a life full of trauma.
I have overcome poverty and abuse.
I learned about neglect and hurt beyond my years.
I have learned that everyone says they don't care,
but deep down, they do.

I'm a woman who has fought to be here.
I have felt fear of living and fear of death.
I have seen God's grace and mercy
when none should have been given.
I have seen God pull people from the pits
and place them on the mountaintop.
I have seen people be redeemed and humbled in a single step.
I have felt God near, yet so far away.

I have stayed in places I should never have been.
I have strayed to places I should never have seen.
I'm a child of God with a free spirit.
I have roamed from place to place, trying to find myself.

I'm lost in a world so demanding.
The world pulls me in other directions, leaving me confused,
trying to make sense of it all.
I'm lost in a world I don't belong to, yet I call it home.
I'm hanging on by a thread to a life
I'm not even sure I belong in.

Who am I?

I am a child who loved and got hurt.
I'm a girl who never fit in.
I'm a young lady who never knew what life had to offer.

Who am I?

I am all these things and much more.
I'm a lover, a fighter, a determined woman who strives for more.
I'm a dreamer without her dreams.
I'm a child of God in a world so demanding.
I'm living this life the best I can,
yet I know I can give more.

I'm a giver—but a taker, too.
I'm a child who lost her mother,
and a mother who is holding on to her children.

I'm lost in a world so demanding,
but I'm still standing in a life that was meant to be lived.
I've never seen all that this world is made of,
but I've longed to see the beauty it has to offer.

I'm a child who has roamed but never found a home.
I was made not to fit in,
but also not to stand out.

Who am I?

Questions

Did you love me like a mother should, or were you misunderstood?

Things I want to know but may never be told.

You hold the key to my questions about me, yet these riddles I must beget.

What did you give me? What qualities do I own that were you or are all these mines? Growing up without you, I don't know where I belong, but everyone reassures me that it will get better in time. I need to know how much time it will be before I start feeling like me. The true me, the me who is left behind in a world so defining but yet I'm limitless. As I grow and learn, I'm the child of loneliness. I started to create a life out of love, or so I thought. I have kids just to have a family of my own. Just to belong, just to love like I know I could. Echoes of you still hunt me because you're not here to share the family ties. I try to do the best I can, but I'm always lacking in my skills I should have learned from you. I'm lacking in being a woman but yet I'm a woman. Questions are all I have, and no answers to make me understand.

I'm Struggling

I'm struggling to survive!
I'm struggling to live!
I'm struggling to discover who I am.
I'm fighting to let go,
but holding on to a lie I was always told.

I am a dreamer who never achieved her dreams—
a lost soul traveling back and forth
between limbo and a world of the living.

I'm struggling to see what God has for me.
I see the pain in their eyes,
and I don't understand why.
I see no hope to thrive.
I'm struggling to live life that way.
I'm struggling to stay,
but don't know where to go.

What do you do when you lose your soul?
Who do you know that will revive it
when all hope is lost?

I'm struggling to find my place
when God has called me to stand
and face the troubles of this world.
I'm struggling to let my light shine.
I'm struggling—
and yet I say I'm fine.

When will I learn to stop being so kind?
I'm struggling with always being knocked down.

God, I'm struggling…
and I don't know how to stop it!

Death Destroys

Death waits for no one.
It knocks on the door,
and once it's let in,
it will destroy you from the inside out.

Death will tear apart families and friends,
making life seem chaotic—
as if your heart is being stabbed by a knife.

Death will take over
and scare you with the unknown—
what's to come,
and where you will go.

Death waits for no one.

Death will leave you alone
and make you feel lonely.
It will call your name
and hold you near,
but never call you home.

It will allow you to stay in limbo
while life goes on around you,
and you never know where you should be.

Death will feed you lies
and make you see life in a new, darker way.
It will make you part of a club
you never wanted to join.

It will take away your identity
and make you lose your way.
It is what fear is made of—
what life has warned us about.

Death will harden your heart
and make you never want to love again.
It will rob you of your joy
and make you believe
that life can't go on
while you hold on
to the shattered dreams
and the never-ever-again.

Death is not what we want to know,
but we all will face it
in our lives of hope.

I'm Worthy

I'm worthy of love, of being thought of,
Though all my life I was told I'd never be enough.
The enemy whispered, and I believed the lie,
That I was alone in a crowd, unseen to every eye.

I waited in silence, never called by name,
Letting others tear me down, drowning in shame.
I grew cold to the world, for too long I was wronged,
I carried their cruelty and held it too strong.

How could people kill the light inside me,
Try to bury my spirit, blind who I might be?
As a teen, I turned from the Lord in despair,
"How could a just God allow so much carelessness there?"

I never looked upward, never lifted a prayer,
Through pain and through weeping, I thought He wasn't there.
I believed He was silent, that He didn't hear,
That His love was absent, His heart wasn't near.

So, I hit rock bottom, with nowhere to go,
Stuck in my sin, in my sorrow, my woe.
No one to lean on, no ear, no embrace,
Just emptiness pressing, no comfort, no grace.

I wanted to end it, to silence it all,
Convinced no one cared if I stumbled or fall.
With a gun in my hand and despair in my mind,
I cried out to a God I thought I'd never find.

On my knees, I pleaded, "Lord, hear my prayer.
Please let me feel You, please show me You care.
For I am too broken, too far, too undone—
If You'll love me still, let Your mercy be won."

And in that moment, His presence broke through,
The God I'd rejected said, "I've always loved you."
I'd known of His stories, the words, and the name,
But never the Person who carried my shame.

I thought I was worthless, but God proved me wrong,
He'd been with me in silence, with me all along.
The darkness had smothered, tried to snuff out my flame,
But His hand protected, He called me by name.

Now I've learned this light must be nurtured, kept near,
For the enemy seeks to erase it with fear.
But God's love is greater—it heals and restores,
It welcomes the broken, it opens new doors.

You will never be perfect, yet He loves you still,
Through every hard valley, His grace will fulfill.
So remember this truth when the night presses in:
You're worthy, beloved, forgiven of sin.

I'm worthy. I'm loved. My heart can declare:
The God who redeemed me will always be there.

My Story

As I sit and listen to the rain call my name,
The pain from within is brought to life once again.
The hurt of yesterday is still there—
lurking and waiting.
It is there to destroy my heart and my peace.

Lord, life has not been fair.
I have learned to let go and stand alone,
but you have called me to tell it all from the rooftop.

How can I look into the eyes of judgmental people
and tell my story?
I trust you—and only you.
People have hurt me, time and time again,
and yet I must open up and tell it all.

I do not know what you want me to do,
but I have heard Your call.
As I wait anxiously for You to tell me which way to go,
I feel my heart drop to the ground.

Can I expose myself and be that vulnerable before Your
people?
Can I tell my story—the one that led me to Your steeple?

I can tell them how you found me.
I am a weak human with many downfalls,
but I'm holding on to Your every word.

I am trying to learn my place in the body of Christ,
but it's hard when all I see
is everyone around me trying to knock me down.

The devil says I am not good enough,
and I will never make it.
He whispers sweet nothings

into my brothers' and sisters' ears.
He tries his hardest to drag them underground.
He rips children from their mothers and fathers
and makes them feel like You are nowhere to be found.

He takes the biggest man down
and makes us feel like we can't do it alone.
He lies to us
and tries to trick us into believing
that the church is the reason people have turned their
backs.

Life on earth is chaotic,
and we are waiting for our heavenly crowns.
We need the blood of Jesus
to flood us with His love—right now.

Lost identity.

I am fighting to live
I am fighting to breathe
I am fighting for the love that used to be.

Life is not what it seems.

I am fighting for you and me.
I am fighting between the dream and reality.
I am losing my grip on me.
I am fading in the background, never to be seen.
I lost my identity trying to be what you wanted me to be.
I am fighting to live
I am fighting to breathe
I am fighting for the love that used to be.
Till I have no fight left in me.

Canceled

Canceled plans,
canceled dreams!
Out in no man's land,
trying to figure out who we are made to be.

Living a life that was given to me,
not truly seeing the beauty surrounding us.

Dreams made of smoke
that quickly fade away.
Reality sets in
as time slips from our grips.

Falling for the lies we are fed,
not knowing how to just be.
Not knowing if we will ever achieve
the best we believe we deserve.

Letting life go on—
with canceled plans
and shattered dreams
of what was to be.

How is something so simple
made into a complicated scheme?

Canceled plans.
Canceled dreams.

I'm Lost

I'm a lost soul who has been wandering around,
just living but not existing.
I lost myself in the chaos of living,
giving away pieces of me to people who couldn't care less.

I must confess,
I let my dreams fly away in the wind, never to be achieved.
I let go of who I was
and became who you wanted me to be.

I'm worth more than I sold my soul for.
I try to show the love,
but how can you stand still when your world is falling apart?

This heart of mine has always been so kind,
but has stopped caring
after so long of being stabbed in the back
by the people who claim to love you.

I went through more stuff than I can tell you,
and my story is so long
it can't be told in a short period of time.

I grew up knowing dysfunction
and being familiar with mental abuse,
but never knew it was a crime.

I knew religion,
but not God.

Life taught me to follow the rules
and not to question what I was told.

When I started to think for myself,
I risked the opportunity of becoming an outcast.

I caught so many lies told,
but not enough truth to behold.

I lost people I loved

and learned to be alone.

I let go of the family ties
and planted my own roots in this world—
set apart from the family curses.

I broke the chains,
all in Jesus' name.

I learned who God is
and never doubt where I belong.

But my heart breaks
for all the people I love
who hide away from God above.

The pain they feel,
the hurt they experience—
because of someone who claimed God's name.

That is not what God wanted
or what He had planned for your life.
But your heart went to stone.

God knew you before you were born,
but you went another way—
the path that destroys who you were made to be.

Fighting

I'm fighting to live.
I'm fighting to breathe.
I'm fighting this anxiety.
I'm fighting for the love that used to be.
I'm fighting to give you parts of me.
I'm fighting not to leave—
but I have no fight left in me.

I'm trying to hold on to your promises,
but I'm failing to understand
this load that has been put on me.

I'm fighting for you and me—
can't you see?

I'm fighting to live.
I'm fighting to breathe.
I'm fighting this anxiety.
I'm fighting for the love that used to be.

I'm fighting with myself
when God said, *"Let it be."*

Death

Death lingers in my life
and holds on to me like it has a place here with
me.
Its touch tingles on my heart, knowing it tore us
apart.
It walks side by side with me, taunting me of an
early demise.
My mother died at a young age, but does that
mean I will too?
Death plays its tricks in my mind,
holding onto the memories of you,
but knowing they are starting to fade away.

Death laughs at me and starts to haunt me in my
every day.
What do you say to death when all you want
is to be set free from his grasp?
He tightens his hand around your throat,
making it harder to breathe.

The memory of you starts to fade away.
What can I do, or do I have to let go?
Death is all I will ever know.

Unlovable One

In the quiet corners of my heart,
Where shadows whisper, doubts reside,
I wonder if I'm set apart,
Destined always to be denied.

Eyes that see but never stay,
Hands that touch but never hold,
Lips that kiss then drift away,
Leaving me in the cold.

I yearn for warmth, for love's embrace,
But find me alone instead,
A solitary, empty space,
Where hope is filled with dread.

Is it me, this broken shell,
That others see and turn away?
A silent scream, a private hell,
Where longing keeps the light at bay.

I try to smile, to play the part,

To hide the cracks within my soul,
But every beat of my fragile heart,
Reminds me of this endless toll.

In dreams, I find a fleeting peace,
A world where love might come to stay,
But waking brings no sweet release,
Just another lonely day.

So here I stand, the unlovable one,
With weary eyes and heavy sigh,
Waiting for the rising sun,
To chase the darkness from my sky.

For maybe in the light of dawn,
A tender hand will reach for me,
And in that touch, I'll be reborn,
Loved at last, and finally free

It's Terminal

The doctor says it's terminal.
There is no resolution to your problem.
You are on your way out of this cruel world,
and you don't have a lot of time left.

They leave you alone in your hospital bed
to face your health and diagnosis on your own.
Your heart is broken,
and there is no one who can stop the pain you are facing.

The grieving begins—
but it's not for you,
it's for all the things you won't be there to experience.

Your children will grow up
and never know your struggle.
They will never know
how much you love them
or what you wish for their lives.

You can't write down all these emotions
for what they'll go through in their life.
What do you say to them
as they have to live on—
while you just die?

I can't tell them
how much it breaks my heart
to not be there
when they walk down the aisle,
or when they have their first child.

I can't just say, "I'm sorry,"
and pretend it will all be alright.

Yes, time will go on,
and you won't hurt as badly
as you did when I first die.

Time won't heal everything—

but it will distract you from the pain.

Life will be a roller coaster
full of surprises—
some good,
some heartbreaking.

Life will grab you by the shirt
and make you want to cry.
And you will.

It's terminal.
And I'm going to die.

This is your final goodbye.

Look me in the eyes
and tell me how unfair life is—
but don't you dare cry.

You will have time
to go through the emotions,
and when you do,
I'll already be on the other side.

Know this:
I love you with all my soul.
And I really did try.

I tried to live this life for you,
but I couldn't keep holding on
to the lies my body told.

I had to let go of my struggles
and go home—
where I will finally be at peace.

Anger

Anger flows out of my pores;
it is within my core.
My heart has turned to stone
because of the anger I hold.

I'm angry you left me alone.
I'm angry God took you home.
I'm angry
and I have nowhere to go.
I'm angry
and I can't stop it from growing.

I'm angry,
and there is nothing you can do.
I'm turning away
from the only ways I know.

I must live this life without you.
I'm angry beyond my years.
Will anyone ever care?

I'm angry at the family
who pretend to be there.
I'm angry at you.
I'm angry at the world,
and I don't know what to do.

Growing Up

I grew up in a different time than now.
Time flew by
as I sat with my old soul.

I was told I was grown beyond my years,
but I'm a child
with years to go.

My inner child now knows
I was robbed of my childhood—
with broken promises
and no one to protect me from the hood.

I will grow up far from where I started,
but not quite where I should be.

I have a free soul.
It doesn't want to stay,
but doesn't want to go.

My soul is demanding me to listen to it,
for I have left it standing
and depleted it of everything good.

Life has drained me
of everything from within.
I no longer fear the monster under my bed
I now know
the monsters are all around
and don't want me to survive.

God found me dead inside again
and brought me back to life.

This is what it was like growing up for me.

I Don't Belong

I don't belong.
I tried to fit into your world,
but I don't belong.

You opened your house to me,
but I don't belong to your family.

I tried to fit into your world,
but I don't belong.

I have never felt so out of place.
I must go on,
because I cannot stay here anymore.

I don't belong.

I have roamed,
looking for a home,
but I can't find the place I'm supposed to be.

As the years go on,
I'm living in a fantasy,
trying to build my dynasty.

Trying to realize who I am,
and where I belong.
If it's not with you,
then with who?

Life is so fragile—
but so cruel at the same time.
I must move on,
but I can't let go.

Where should I go?
Trauma is all I know.

Life moves on
while I stay stuck and all alone.
Life moves on,
but there's no one home.

The lights have been turned off in the house,
and the pain has taken over
the love that was once there.

I don't belong here.

Letting Go

I am letting go of the pain I feel—
the lonely nights of never knowing.
The hurt has consumed my inner parts,
killing me bit by bit.

I looked into your eyes
and no longer saw the love I once knew.
I must let it go before I begin to hate you.

We once loved each other
so deeply and passionately,
but that time has passed us by,
and we must let go
to see where we are supposed to be.

I am letting go of the idea of you and me,
and the dreams that were dreamt for us.
My heart cannot hold on to a dying love
that will not move forward
but clings to the past.
I do not live there anymore.
I must let go
to allow my heart to flow to its own beat once more.

Love is a funny thing,
and I must learn
that not everyone is meant to be a holder of it.

I have never felt true love.
I have loved and been loved,
but never held someone's heart in my hands
that was all mine.

You see, each time we love,
we leave pieces of our hearts behind—
never to completely fulfill
the one desire of being the only one.

Dreaming

I'm dreaming of when life was so carefree.
When all my fears were nothing compared to
now.

Dreaming of the places I would go and see.
I'm dreaming of a future so bright
that no one can snuff this light.

I'm dreaming of a world
without pain and sorrow for me.
I'm dreaming of tomorrow
and what it will bring.

I'm dreaming of a love so true,
it must be a dream.

I'm dreaming of my future,
without a clue of what to do.
I'm dreaming
when I should be living my dreams.

The Motherless Daughter

The greatest pain I ever knew was losing my mother.
The world became an unknown place for me.
I no longer belonged or fit into the scheme of living.
I became the motherless daughter.

I no longer had a connection to this world,
but I had nowhere to go.
My family tree branch was broken
and no longer allowed family ties to grow.

The sad thing about losing your mom
her family disappears.
You are left wondering what you did.

Time goes on, and relationships grow thin.
Soon, you grow up and start a family of your own.
You cannot connect to the women around you,
for you are broken.

You will try but can never relate.
You will grow a relationship with your daughter,
and you will rewrite some of those family traditions
but there is still a lot missing.

You will never fit in,
and you will understand it's because
you are a motherless daughter.

God, Where Are You?

God, where are you in the time I need you the
most?
How can life kick my butt and leave me barely
hanging on?
I'm not sure I want to live anymore.
God, where are you?

I lost my foundation at an early age,
and I lost myself inside the streets
because I had nothing else.
God, where are you in this chaos I made?

Life is beating me at this game called life.
I don't know where to go
or what to let go.

Where are you, God?
You called me to you at a young age,
but I let go of your hold in my teens
because I couldn't see through the pain in my
eyes.

Now I'm crying out one more time
God, where are you in this chaos called life?

Cloud of Grief

The cloud of grief consumes you.
Holds you in limbo, not knowing what is next for you.
The cloud of grief comes in the night and takes all your light out
of you.
It leaves you vulnerable and exposed to everyone around you.

The love for the person that you lost is so intense,
it is all you know.
The cloud of grief consumes you and won't let you go.

The cloud of grief lingers over you, years after you thought you
let go.
Grief wraps you in its embrace,
only to have the cloud of grief hang over your head like a black
cloud,
raining down on you, just in case you thought you could be free
from this sad tragedy.

The cloud of grief has control over you,
and everyone gives you the pity eye.
When all you want to do is cry out, "I'm okay! I'm fine!"
But they all know it's lies.

Lies that will carry you through life,
as everyone around you doesn't know what to say to you.
The cloud of grief is all you will know—
until you learn to process the loss you feel.

Fragile

Life is so fragile,
a thin line between living and breathing.

Too scared to live, but too poor to move.
How can you deny the soul a chance to survive?

We're too afraid to be kind,
but we live in our minds.

Life is so fragile;
everything can change in the blink of an eye.

All the lies we say and all the stories we tell
can't get us by.

Life is fragile,
a thin line between living and breathing.

Life is so fragile,
and yet we are holding on to the edge of our existence
and denying our souls.

Life is so fragile,
and yet we are not living, just existing in a world so cold.

Life is so fragile,
but needs to be lived... is what I'm told.

Look into My Eyes!

You looked me in my eyes and still chose to lie.

How can I rely on you when you can't even tell me the truth?

What do you think I will do? Wilt away or die from your lies?
Let me tell you. I'm a survivor, and I will go on with or without you.

So, stop right there and don't say another word, because I will not allow you to tear me down anymore.

You had your chance. You had your turn.
And all you did was prove to me that I shouldn't let you in.

How dare you try to turn this on me
when your actions spoke louder than the words you spoke?

So, goodbye and farewell are all I can say,
you never loved me anyway.

Every Blank page is a beginning.

What Is Love?

Love is a verb.
It's a word of action and compassion,
but it can build you up
or tear you down.

Love can reach the darkest places in your soul,
but it can also cause that darkness to grow.

It can light up your world
and make your dreams come alive.
Love is said to be known
by every culture in the world,
yet it has killed more hearts
than any war.

Love is best felt
with every beat of your heart and soul.
But to be real,
it will hurt
and deny you any right to own it.

Love is the purest emotion known to humankind,
yet the sharpest blade to your insides.
With every swipe of that knife,
it will rip you open
and spit you out.

Love will make you vulnerable
beyond your imagination.
It will whisper sweet everything's in your ear
while sleeping with your best friend.

Love is not what we were taught.
Love is chaos,
yet the calm in your life.

It's what we all want to feel,
yet the hardest thing for us to nurture and grow.
Love will make us stay
when we really should go.

Love is the way we get abused and used,
but for love's sake,
we don't mind.

Love can turn hearts to stone
and flip your world upside down in no time at all.
It will make you believe you can fly
when you're really tied up and caged.

Love will gently touch your mind,
and you'll have no idea at all.

Earthly love is not kind.
Godly love is divine,
so different than earthly love.

In time,
you'll see this…
was not love at all.

Back to Me

I look into your eyes as our bodies intertwine.
You say I'm the only one,
but we both know
you'll be at her house later.

You've twisted my vision.
I used to see through you.
Now I can't see past the lies you fed me.
I stay, enduring the abuse,
knowing I don't belong here.
Still, I hold on to a tiny sliver of hope,
knowing it's me who will be the one
bleeding all over everything.

I'm not loved,
but I keep believing one day you might.
I'm broken deep in my soul,
and I know only God can put me back together.

I've walked this road long enough to know
where I'm headed if I keep going.
Still, I step forward, again and again,
even as I whisper,
I do not belong here.

Can I really go back?
Back to the true me.
the one who once believed in love,
the one who didn't know what abuse was,
who hadn't yet allowed you
to lay your hands on her.

My mind races
as the truth settles in:
You no longer hold me.

Little by little,
I am being set free.
Free to move forward.
In twenty years,
You'll still be in this same place,
trapped in the prison you created
and called a life.

But not me.

I will soar
above the pain you caused.
I will heal
from the abuse you inflicted.
And most of all,
God will heal the trauma
I carried
while I stood beside you
and helped build you up.

Now, I'm building myself.

Survivor

I am a survivor.

I survived when I should have died.

I fought to be here.

I chose to live instead.

I'm a survivor.

Maybe I'm stubborn, but I'm a survivor.

I chose to live when death was near.

I'm a survivor, and I fought to be here.

I Don't Know What to Say

I don't know what to say or what to do.
I looked deep within and told everything.
Life is so hard right now, but where do I belong when everything
I know is gone?
I don't know what to say to you when life as we know it has
changed.

I am sorry for your loss, but the scars you will carry your whole
life.
I have become the heavy that no one knows how to carry.
No one can look me in my eyes and be genuine with me.
I have become a burden that no one knows how to understand.
No one knows what to say or what to do.

Look at me and be real with me.
Stop pitying my life and be my friend.
I can't take it anymore.
I don't know what to say or what to do when everyone tries to
avoid me because they can't handle sad.

I became the star of this tragedy.
I am mad at everyone and can't stand the look,
and the cowardly way out you gave me.

Look at me.
I am the motherless daughter that you are afraid of.

Let's Talk

Let's talk about our lives of tragedy and compare our stories.
You know we belong to the same club.
We are the children of misfortune, and no one knows how to relate to us.
We have become the misfits who do not fit in.

Let's talk about our misfortune and how the cards we were dealt
left us in a rut. Life has been interesting with the waves of misfortune on our side.
We are chewed up and spit out in this life.
We hear the lies and see that luck is not on our side.

Let's talk about life and our dreams that we hold in our hearts,
but the life we live is no charity case ,you and me.
Let's talk about this life that we were given.

I Will Overcome

I will beat the odds and overcome poverty and misfortune.
I will keep my head high and overcome what you thought my
future would hold.
I will live a life out of the norm, but I will not let your stats hold
me down.

I am not what you decide my life will hold, but what God has
given me to try.
Your lies will become my reason why. I will overcome this life of
misfortune.

I am sorry that I will not stay here to wither and die like you
wanted me to.
I will soar above your expectations and achieve more than you
thought I could.
I am not a victim of the streets, but the product of an overcomer.

God has ordained me to a life of peace, and I will not let you
steal my joy anymore.
I will overcome what you thought I would never be able to all in
God's name.

So, sit back and watch me soar beyond your dreams of what I
could do,
and watch me overcome the lies you set down for me.

No More

I won't plea.
I won't beg for you to be in my life.
I'm worth more than the lack of love you show me.
I won't ask you to stay, and I won't cry any tears.
I will stand strong and know I did nothing wrong.
I loved you and tried to say family is everything, but some family is toxic.

I just need to let go and move on.
I can't hold on to a false hope of being family once more.
From now on, I will say you were someone I once knew,
and I won't blink a lash.

For nothing lasts, and nothing holds strong.
Blood is nothing and doesn't make us family.
For family stands for forever.

Must I love you?

Dreamer

I am the dreamer who dreamt of a life so far from where I started.
I dreamt a dream of getting out of the streets to live a life of peace and joy.
I was always told that life was not for me, but for everyone else.
I was told I would always suffer and have a life of misfortune to carry me through the life I was given.

I am sorry your lies did not hold me back like you thought they would.
I soared over your expectations and became the woman God wanted me to be.
I am the dreamer whose dreams are coming true.
God has blessed me more than you can ever know.

I am sorry your scheme didn't work in my life.
God made me a dreamer to show others they can reach their goals when no one else believes in them.
I am a dreamer of life, and I have overcome the lies you told.

Streets

In the heart of the city where life pulses strongly,
lies a network of pathways where souls belong.
The streets whisper tales of joy and pain,
of hope and despair, like a never-ending refrain.

Concrete rivers winding through the urban sprawl,
connecting lives, big and small.
Footsteps echo on the hard ground,
A symphony of movement, a bustling sound.

Neon lights flicker, painting shadows long,
as the city dances to its own sweet song.
From bustling avenues to quiet lanes,
each street tells a story that forever remains.

In the alleyways, hidden from the sun's bright gaze,
Secrets linger in the shadows, in a mysterious haze.
The graffiti on the walls, a form of art,
A voice of the streets, a beating heart.

Through the seasons, the streets stand strong,
witnessing the passage of time, right and wrong.
They hold the memories of those who came before,
their whispers in the wind, a haunting lore.

Teen Years

I thought I was grown and pretended that I knew what I was
doing,
but truth be told, I hadn't a clue.
These are the teen years, and what I went through
I can never tell you.

My teen years are colored with death and sorrow beyond my
years.
Trying to survive but running away every chance, I got.
Not belonging or having a spot.
My teen years were not what I thought.

I grew up beyond my years,
trying to love when I didn't know how.
My teen years let me run wild and free,
and I couldn't be tamed, or so I thought.

My teen years were full of mistakes and bad decisions.
A drink or two that took me down a road I never knew.
I learned a thing or two.

My teen years had me running wild and free,
never to be tamed, or so I thought.
These were my teen years.
I will never be the same.

Neglect

In the silence of neglect's cold embrace,

Lies a world of sorrow, a hidden place,

Where hearts grow heavy, spirits dim,

Lost in the shadows, hope grows thin.

A child unnoticed, longing for care,

Invisible tears, a soul laid bare,

Yearning for love, for a gentle touch,

Neglected, forgotten, feeling so much.

Words left unspoken, actions failed,

In neglect's grip, innocence is veiled,

Lonely cries in the dead of night,

Echoes of neglect, a haunting plight.

Like a flower wilting without sun,

Neglect's damage can't easily be undone,

Aching souls wounded and worn,
In the darkness, feeling so forlorn.

But in the midst of neglect's cruel sting,
There lies a chance for hearts to sing,
For kindness and empathy to heal,
To mend the broken, to help them feel.

Tribe

In the vast expanse of life's great quest,

We search for souls who know us best,

To find our tribe, our kindred spirits,

Whose presence uplifts, whose bond inherits.

Through the noise and chaos of the crowd,

We seek connections strong and proud,

A tribe that sees us, understands our core,

Where we can be ourselves and explore.

In the dance of fate, we find our kin,

Bound by shared values deep within,

Kindred souls who light our way,

Through every night and every day.

Each member is unique, yet hearts are aligned,

In this tribe, true connections bind,

Laughter shared, tears embraced,

In this sacred space, we find our place.

God's Angels

In life's journey filled with twists and turns,

God sends angels, in human form, for us to discern.

They come as friends, mentors, strangers passing by,

Guiding lights to help us reach the sky.

With compassion in their hearts and kindness in their eyes,

They lift us up when our spirit cries.

In moments of darkness, they bring the light,

Showing us the way, shining so bright.

They listen without judgment, understand without words,

Their presence is strong, like the singing of birds.

They walk beside us through joy and through sorrow,

Giving hope for a better tomorrow.

These souls are gifts, rare and true,

Sent by God to help us through.

Their love is a beacon, unwavering and strong,

In their embrace, we always belong.

cherish these blessings, these angels so dear,

For they make the path ahead crystal-clear Grateful for the people
God puts in our way,

Guiding us, supporting us day by day.

Mother

In the silent shadows of sorrow's embrace,

I mourn the loss of your loving grace.

A mother's touch, a guiding light,

Now lost to me in endless night.

Your laughter echoes in memories past,

Fading whispers, too fleeting to last.

Gone too soon, your spirit flies,

Leaving me with tear-stained eyes.

The world feels empty, a hollow place,

Without your smile, without your grace.

In dreams, I seek your gentle hand,

But wake to find only drifting sand.

Each day I carry the weight of my loss,

A heavy burden, a crushing cross.

Yet in my heart, your love remains,

A beacon of hope in life's harsh chains.

Though you've left this earthly shore,

In my soul, you'll live forevermore.

I'll cherish the moments we once shared,
And know your love will always be there.

So, rest in peace, dear mother mine,
In the arms of a love divine.
Your spirit soars, forever free,
And in my heart, you'll always be.

Children

In the garden of innocence, where laughter freely flows,

Lies a world of wonder, where a child's spirit glows.

With eyes full of wonder and hearts pure and bright,

Children dance through life, like stars in the night.

Their laughter like music, a joyful symphony,

Their curiosity boundless, an endless journey.

In their small hands, they hold dreams so grand,

With imaginations wild, they paint life's grandstand.

They see magic in the mundane, beauty in the small,

In their simple joys, find wonder in it all.

With each new discovery, a universe unfurls,

In the eyes of a child, the essence of the world.

Their hearts are full of kindness, their love knows no
end,

In their innocence and joy, they teach us to mend.

They remind us of hope, of dreams yet untold,

In the presence of children, our spirits unfold.

cherish the children, our treasures so dear,

For in their laughter and love, our hearts find cheer.

May we nurture their spirits, with care and with grace,

For children are blessings, the future's embrace.

Goodbye mother

In the quiet whispers of memory's embrace,

I hold you close, in a sacred place.

A bond unbroken, though you're not here,

In the echoes of loss, I shed a tear.

Your laughter lingers in the gentle breeze,

Your love surrounds me, puts my heart at ease.

But in the shadows of absence, I feel the pain,

Losing you, my mother, like a relentless rain.

Your wisdom guides me through each day,

In the solitude of grief, I find my way.

Though you're gone, your spirit lives on,

In the depths of my soul, where you have drawn.

I feel your presence in the stars above,

A shining light, an eternal love.

Though the ache of loss may never fade,

In my heart, your memories are forever made.

So here I stand, with a heavy heart,

Missing you, my mother, torn apart.

But in the quiet moments, I feel you nearby,

In the beauty of love, forever dear.

The Fire Inside

Anger rises, creeping from deep within,
Leaking through my skin like smoke from a
buried flame.
It presses against the cage I built,
Begging to show the world the parts of me I was
never allowed to be.

I've lived inside your version of me,
Trapped in the shell of your comfort,
Pretending I don't ache to break free.
But this rage, it burns — not wild, but steady —
A slow destruction of all I used to feel.

You dressed up lies and called them love.
You spun illusions and called them care.
And I believed until belief turned bitter.
Now the ember of my love is almost gone.
You asked me to exist — not to feel, not to be.

I'm exhausted.
Tired of burying my truth to preserve your
fantasy.
Tired of swallowing fire just to stay soft.
There's no voice left for compromise.
No warmth left to give.

I am numb now.

Frozen from the heat that once fueled me.
But still — a spark remains.

Look me in the eyes.
Do you see it?
We won't survive another storm.
So tell me — is this the end?
Or are you finally ready to change
Before there's nothing left of me at all?

Anger Within

The anger rises again from within, seeping out
of my pores, threatening to break free from the
prison where I hide it.
It seeks to expose the truth of who I am and who
I once was.
I live in your world, never allowed to be myself,
forced to pretend to be the person you created.
Anger is the fire consuming my soul and body,
stirring its dark tendrils within me.

With every lie you've told and every deceitful
story you've spun,
My love has dwindled to a mere spark, barely
holding on.
I'm told to just exist, never to feel the person
God made me to be.
I can't bear these emotions any longer; I want to
let my humanity slip away with every word you
speak.

I am done with your so-called unwavering love
and your selfish ways.
There is no communication left in me.
What am I to do with this anger at my core,
breaking free to rekindle the flame within?
My passion and compassion have died.
Numbness has taken over, cooling my emotions

until I feel nothing.

Look into my eyes and tell me you realize we
won't survive another war.
Is this finally goodbye?
Or can you truly change before you tear my
heart apart?

Memories of You

The memories of you haunt my dreams at night.
Wishing I could call out to you once again and hold your hand.
The memories of you linger inside my head where you now live,
saying I am not enough to love.

The memories of you on this earth are supposed to be cherished,
but have become my nightmares, my emotions I cannot show. I
must hide them inside and lock them in this bottle so no one can
ever know who I am, because that is what you taught me to do.

You taught me to never express my inner parts because they are
not enough. But could you be wrong? Could my heart of gold be
the very thing that tears your lies at the seam?

I hid myself behind these walls and barricaded my emotions so
long, I don't know how to express my hurt to anyone, because I
was taught to never show my emotions. After all, that is how you
become strong.

All I can say is this: **that is wrong**, and being honest makes you
stronger than not feeling your inner parts.

The guilt that arises from going against what I was taught is
enough to drive me crazy, but I know I'm healing.

In the quiet, I still exist

Still, I Stayed

I look into your eyes as our bodies intertwine.
You say I'm the only one
but we both know you'll be at her house later.

You've screwed up my view.
I used to see through you.
Now I can't see past the lies you told me.
I stay and endure the abuse,
knowing deep down I don't belong here.
Still, I hold on to a tiny sliver of hope,
knowing I'll be the one who ends up bleeding
all over everything.

I'm not loved,
but I believe that one day, you will.
I'm broken all through my soul,
and I know no one can put me back together
but God Himself

I've walked this road long enough
to know exactly where I'm headed
if I continue down this path of destruction.
Yet I keep stepping—
Over and over—
Knowing I do not belong here.
But can I really go back?

Back to the real me.
Back to who I used to be.
Back to the love I know I deserve.
Back to a time when none of this made sense,
when I didn't know what abuse was.
Back to the days before I allowed you
to put your hands on me.

My mind races as the reality sets in:
You no longer have a hold on me.
Little by little, I'm being set free
To move on in life.

In 20 years, you'll still be right here
Stuck in the same spot,
Living in the trap you call a life.
But not me.

I will soar above the pain you caused.
I will heal from the abuse I endured.
And most of all,
God will heal the trauma
That came from standing beside you
While I helped build you up
As you slowly tore me down

Left With Nothing but Silence

Abuse is all around me.
I see what it did,
how it twisted my truth,
manipulated my mind,
and made me believe I wasn't worth anything.

The thing about abuse is,
it's not just bruises and broken skin.
Sometimes, the deepest wounds
are the ones no one sees.
Emotional abuse?
It whispers louder than fists ever could.
It silences your voice,
drowns out your worth,
and leaves you
with no words
to lift you up,
no love
to build your soul.

You're left with
emptiness.
Echoes.
Doubt.
And a hollow version of the person you used to be.

Vulnerable

I can't be vulnerable in a world so cold.
I cannot show you the weakest parts of me,
not knowing if you can be trusted.

I cannot be vulnerable and let you see me.
I have been destroyed by people
who said they loved me.

Yet I must be vulnerable.

God,
I cannot expose myself to this world without You.
Can I open up my inner parts
and let You see within my heart?
Can I show You the hurt I endured
for the sake of peace?

To be vulnerable is to be free—
but why is it the scariest thing to do?

I'm me.
Nothing else.

Yet I have seen the evil in this world,
and I have felt pain
no one should ever endure.

I'm me.
And nothing else.

Can I be vulnerable…
and show you?

Becoming a Woman

Blossoming into womanhood,
I once thought myself mature.
Yet today, I embrace the truth:
It's time to shed my childish allure.

No more games of make-believe,
No more clinging to my youth.
Today marks the day I must receive
The mantle of adulthood, in all its truth.

Facing the unknown with grace,
I step into this new role I must play,
Seeking wisdom in each embrace,
Learning how to navigate each new day.

No manual nor guide in hand,
I navigate this uncharted land.
With courage, I shall take my stand,
Embracing my destiny, oh so grand.

I Surrendered to God

I surrendered to God today.
I asked Him to take it all away,
all the hurt, all the pain.

I couldn't hold on to it anymore.
My face is stained with the tears of everything.
I am no longer strong,
and I don't want to try anymore.

God, I surrender it all to You.
I no longer want to hold onto it.
I can no longer carry it in my soul.

God, I surrender it all to You.
Do what you will,
or what you may,
to stop this from consuming me.

I give my burdens to You,
and I know you will help me carry them.

God, I surrender it all to You.
Heal me from within.
Restore what they destroyed.
Bring me back to life again,
and let me feel my passion.

Lead me to where I am supposed to be.
I give it all to you today.
Let it be Yours—
and let it glorify You.

God, I surrendered it all to You.

Ride or die

In the realm of loyalty, a bond so strong,
Ride or die companions, we belong.
Through trials and triumphs, we stand tall,
Together we rise, never to fall.

In the depths of darkness, you're my light,
Through stormy seas, we navigate right.
Hand in hand, we face the tide,
Ride or die, side by side.

Through fire and ice, we brave the test,
In the journey of life, we give our best.
With unwavering trust, our souls entwine,
Ride or die, a bond divine.

In the battlefield of life, we fight as one,
With courage and valor, our battles won.

Through thick and thin, come what may,

Ride or die, come what may.

 here's to us, in unity strong,

Ride or die, where we belong.

In the tapestry of destiny, by each other's side,

Ride or die, with hearts open wide.

Marriage

In the dance of two souls, a union divine,

A vow spoken in love, an eternal sign,

Bound together in heart and mind,

In the sacred bond of marriage, we find.

Through trials and triumphs, hand in hand,

Together we walk on life's shifting sand,

Building a future, strong and grand,

In the shelter of our love, a steadfast band.

Each day a journey, a shared quest,

Through joys and sorrows, we're put to the test,

Yet in each other, we find our best,

In the sanctuary of marriage, we are blessed.

Two hearts beating as one, in harmony,

Love binds us together, softly, endlessly, eternally.

Finding church

In the whispers of the wind, a gentle call,

Back to the church, where spirits enthrall.

Lost in the shadows, but seeking the light,

Finding your way back through the darkest night.

Through the doors of faith, a welcome embrace,

In the sanctuary of love, find your place.

Forgiveness and grace, in abundance, flow,

In the arms of the church, let your spirit grow.

Tears may fall, as you kneel and pray,

In the presence of God, find your way.

Broken pieces mend, hearts anew,

In the healing presence, faith is renewed.

Guided by hope, in the choir's song,

In the harmony of faith, you belong.

With open arms, the congregation waits,

In the fellowship of the church, open gates.

Embracing the journey, with faith restored,

In the sacred space, find the Lord.

For in the heart of the church, you'll see,

A path of love and grace, forever free.

walk with courage, in the light divine,

In the sanctuary of faith, let your spirit shine.

Finding your way back to the church's embrace,

In the journey of faith, find solace and grace.

Boy to a Man

My heart melts to see you grow,
to learn the things you now know.

As time goes on, you'll grow so fast,
so quickly—
and before we know it, you'll be on your own.

We'll try to make the memories last.
We'll laugh at the past
but move forward to the future.

In my heart, you will always be my baby boy—
the one who once didn't know how to do anything,
who depended on me to love and care for him.

The one who was always there,
trying to learn everything I did.

The boy who overcame his fears,
who started to crawl,
then began to walk,
and never stopped there.

You grew into a boy
who climbed the trees outside,
as I watched patiently,
waiting to see you grow into yourself.

Then came the young man.
The one who may think he's grown,
but we both know there's still more time to go.

And before we even realize it...
You become a man
right in front of our eyes.

In my son , I hear echoes of my heart learning to love beyond itself.

Baby Girl

Baby girl, where has the time gone?
It feels like just yesterday
you were wrapped in my arms—
tiny, wild, and full of wonder.

You have always been my baby girl,
the one whose heart is made of fire and ice.
You feel deeply, love wholeheartedly,
and give more than most could ever understand.

You carry a strength that runs deep,
even when you don't see it in yourself.
Your light is radiant.
Don't ever let this world dim your sparkle.

There will be people who won't understand you,
who may try to silence your fire
or dull your shine,
but don't you dare shrink.

Take care of your spirit.
Nurture your heart.
Speak your truth with love.
And always remember,
you were created with purpose,
with a calling that only you can fulfill.

You are stronger than you know,
braver than you believe,
and more loved than you'll ever realize.

No matter what pain you face,
no matter how heavy the world feels,
God will be right there with you.

He sees you.
He hears you.
He holds every tear.

Just turn to Him.
Give Him your fears,
your dreams,
your heart.
Let Him guide you.

Baby girl,
you are a masterpiece in progress.
And I will always be proud of the woman you're becoming.

Always.
Forever.
My baby girl.

Growing Into Me

I am growing into who I am supposed to be.
I learned to tame the dysfunction, for it has no
place here with me.
I learned to love and forgive and to be free.
I am growing into myself for my family.

I see what dysfunction does and how it starts a
chain reaction.
I refuse to let it continue on.
It will stop with me.

I am learning to be strong and heal from within.
I am growing into myself.

I am learning how to love my family
and how to let them grow.
I am healing for my family.
I am growing into myself.

Growth is the echo of yesterday's pain blooming into tomorrow's strength.

Remember When!

Remember when there were only us?
When life showed us love,
and dreams could be real?
The feeling of finally being home in your arms,
love was all we needed.

Remember when we became three instead of
two?
Oh, the memories we created to start this family.
When time held still,
and our hearts felt love they never knew.

Remember the love that grew
and the dreams that we dreamt?
It wasn't a scheme,
it was real.
You and me.

Remember the chaos we thought
was all we would ever know,
as our child grew
the chaos of life and living.
What a life we lived.

Remember when our family grew to four instead
of three,

and our hearts grew ten times their size
to house this love we have?

Remember the memories we created with this
family,
the times spent growing
and loving our children.

Time flew by,
and the chaos faded,
but our family kept living and learning.

Remember when we thought
we would never know this kind of life.

Remember when we fought
to survive and thrive
in a world that left us behind.

**Look at us now,
we survived the hard times.**

Grow

I heard you say that everyone must grow,
but I see so many hold on to the life they know.

To grow is what they say we must do,
but life will knock you down and ask you your name.
If you are not careful,
it will put you in your place and make you obey.

To grow is a word that is made to challenge you,
but you fight with it to stay the same.
You secretly dream in the night,
but you're too scared to grow in the day.

Life has a hold on you,
but you don't let go.
To grow is what they say we must do,
but we're too scared to accept it.

To grow is a beautiful thing,
but we hang on to the life we live,
all in the name of content.

Why is it so hard
to grow into who God made us to be?
To grow is to let go
of what they will say about you.

So, we stay stuck in a world of judgment
instead of growing into who God made us to be.

Let go and grow!

Like roots unseen, I grow quietly reaching always for the light.

God's Grace

In the whispers of the wind, in the dance of the trees,

Lies a grace so divine, carried on a gentle breeze.

It weaves through the fabric of life's intricate lace,

A gift from above, the touch of God's grace.

In moments of darkness, when all seems lost,

It shines like a beacon, no matter the cost.

It lifts up the weary, the broken, the meek,

A soothing balm for the hearts that seek.

It flows like a river, pure and ever bright,

Guiding our steps through the darkest night.

In the silence of dawn, in the song of the birds,

God's grace whispers softly, in comforting words.

It's in the laughter of children, the smile of a friend,

In the warmth of a touch that will never end.

It's a love beyond measure, a light in the storm,

A shelter in chaos, a heart that's warm.

be grateful for this gift so profound,

For in God's grace, true peace is found.

May it fill our hearts, our souls embrace,

Forever and always, in God's loving grace.

The Silence carries what the
heart cannot say.

Life Cycle

Life has a cycle, and we are in the mix.

Life starts out as we are infants.

At this stage, we are lessons for our parents and the dreams of their family.

As we grow and become toddlers, we become part of each parent to annoy the other.

When we become children, we become individuals and make some friends.

We live life with them and learn our hard lessons.

We continue to grow into ourselves and become grown.

If we did it right, we planted some roots and worked towards our dreams.

As our garden of life grows, we should be nurturing those life goals.

Some of us will fall off our life road and get lost along the way.

Others will continue to be content with what life has bestowed on us.

While others will work hard and achieve their life dreams.

Life offers us all the same things, but we each take what we need out of this life cycle.

Life offers us things, but we decide how hard we will thrive.

Life Should Be Lived

Life should be experienced and felt.
Life should be felt from within.

Life should be free—
yet it's costly to me.
Life should hold all your dreams,
yet they are broken beyond repair.

Life is the fiber of our being,
yet we act like we don't care.

To live and dream is to achieve our life goals,
but what if I told you,
life is not supposed to be this way?

Life should be cherished and loved,
but some of us have endured
more pain than one lifetime should hold.

Life can sometimes feel like a knife,
cutting us up.

Life is funny like that.
Some can go through it untouched,
while others are bruised and battered
beyond recognition.

Learning

I'm learning.
I'm learning who you are
and how far you will go.

I'm learning how You have called me to You,
and how You won't let me go.

I'm learning what this life is meant to be,
and how it's supposed to be lived.

You've taught me so much.
But is it enough?

Father

In the gentle strength of a father's embrace,

Lies a love that time and trials can't erase.

A guiding light, a steady hand,

In the journey of life, a rock to stand.

With calloused hands and a heart so kind,

A father's love is a treasure to find.

Through whispered wisdom and silent care,

He weaves a legacy beyond compare.

From childhood dreams to grown-up fears,

A father's presence soothes and clears.

In laughter shared and tears wiped away,

His love shines bright, come what may.

A protector, a mentor, a friend so true,

A father's love is steadfast through and through.

In memories made and stories told,

His presence is more precious than gold.

Life Is Not What It Seems

Life is full of the memories we created,
Full of us fated dreams and our discarded
schemes.
We hold on to everything but let go of
something.

Life is not what it seems.

Life goes on and we pretend we are alright,
But we are really dying inside.
Dying for the love we knew
And the dreams we dreamt when we were
young.

We fell into this routine and lost our souls.
Life is not what it seems.

Living in this chaos we call life.
Where do we go?
How do we get back to ourselves once more?

Life is not what it seems.

The bond between Mother and Daughter.

In the dance of generations, a bond so dear,
Between mother and daughter, crystal clear,
A love that blossoms year by year,
In their hearts, forever nearby.

From the first breath, a profound connection,
Mother and daughter, in love, they're bonded,
A journey of love, in harmony they're found,
In each other's arms, happiness is crowned.

Through laughter and tears, they stand strong,
Mother's wisdom, a beacon lifelong,
Daughter's spirit, a vibrant song,
Together they conquer, together they belong.

So, here's to mothers and daughters, so true,
In their love, the world feels anew,
A bond that forever will renew,
In their hearts, a love that grew.

The Unborn Child

The unborn child cries out,
"Why must I die? Why?"

Who are you to decide my fate in life?
If you prick me, I'll bleed, for my heart does
beat.
Doesn't that make me human?

I'll have little feet and hands,
yet they will never be seen.
And my voice, never to be heard.

How can you end me
before you feel me kick,
before you ever know
what a gift I truly am?

Angel of Mine

Angel of mine,
you were given to us
for a short period of time.

You're now living in heaven,
as we're left behind.
only with a memory
of how you looked
in the time you were alive.

Our hearts ache,
our eyes cry,
our minds wonder why.

As time goes on,
our hearts will start to heal,
but a part of us
will always cry,
tears of sorrow for you,
as we think of what might have been.

Angel of mine.

Goodbye Sister

My heart breaks to know you are no longer here
with me.
Each day, I'm forced to wear a smile and try to
pick up all the pieces.
But what am I supposed to do now that you are
gone?

I'm all alone with no one to talk to.
I reach for the phone but realize you are not a
phone call away anymore.
You will always be my first friend—the one who
was supposed to be there till the end.

With every tear I ever cried,
you were right by my side to catch them all—
until God called you home.
I'm left with this emptiness in my heart,
and the endless memories that live within me,
never to be relived with you.

Broken dreams never to be filled with you.
No new memories to be created.
It's killing me that you're not here
when all my life you were my rock to stand on—
the one who kept the faith
when all I ever wanted to do was give up on
faith.

How can any good come from pain?
Faith wasn't knocking on my door.
Now that is all I have—faith.

I'm lost with nowhere to go,
left facing my fear with all my pain
and tears running down my face.

Till we meet again, dear sister,
just know you will never be forgotten,
and a part of me went with you when you went
home.

Let It Go!

Let it go so you can grow.
Let them know you are no longer accepting that.
Let it go so you can protect your peace.

Life doesn't have to be like that.
Let it go and stand your ground.
You can still love them
and not let them in.

Let it go so you can grow.
Let them say whatever they want.
You no longer have to listen to their words.

Let it go so you can live the life you deserve.
Family ties can be cut.
Let it go so you can grow.

You do not have to allow that in your life.
Let it go so you can love who you are.

Let it go!
So you can grow.

Parenting

Parenting is not for the faint of heart.

You have a child to carry on your family ties,

but you don't realize they will carry on your family curse as well unless you break them in Jesus' name.

Your child will grow under your prayers and strive.

Sometimes they will turn out alright, while other times they will pull your heartstrings and make you cry while asking, "Why?"

Your child will grow up and have their own life, but you will hold on to all the memories you created.

You will discover they sometimes didn't like the way you raised them all this time you thought you did fine.

When you hear their side, will it change how you feel?

Your child will tell you of all the times they deceived you or hid things behind your back.

You will realize parenting was not at all what you thought.

While they are young, embrace this time and enjoy them, because one day you will be on the other side of parenting.

My dearest son

My dear son, my heart's delight,

A beacon of strength, a shining light.

From the moment you entered my life,

You brought me purpose, banished my strife.

With each step you take, each milestone you reach,

My love for you soars, beyond speech.

Your laughter, your courage, fill me with pride,

In your presence, my fears subside.

Through every challenge, every storm,

I'll be your shelter, safe and warm.

I'll stand by you, unwavering and strong,

Guiding you, where you belong.

You are my joy, my greatest treasure,

A bond unbreakable, beyond measure.

As you journey through life's unknown,

Know that in me, you have a mother's home.

 chase your dreams, my precious son,

Know that in me, you've already won.

Wherever you go, whatever you do,

My love for you will always be true.

My dearest daughter

My dearest daughter, my precious one,
A gift of love, like the morning sun.
From the moment you came into my life,
You brought me joy; you eased my strife.

I watched you grow, so pure and true,
A reflection of me, a part of you.
Your laughter, your smile, light up my days,
In your embrace, my heart sways.

Through every triumph, every tear,
I'll stand by you, forever near.
I'll be your rock, your guiding light,
Through the darkest hours of night.

You are my pride, my greatest treasure,
A bond unbreakable, beyond measure.

As you journey through life's winding road,

Know that in me, you have a mother's abode.

 spread your wings, my darling child,

Embrace the world, fierce and wild.

But always remember, wherever you roam,

You'll find love and solace in your mother's home.

Growing Old

In the quiet passage of time, as days
slip away,
We journey through life, where memories sway.
Lines etched on skin, like stories untold,
A tapestry of moments, as we grow old.

The once vibrant hues of youth now fade,
But wisdom and grace in their place have lain.
With each passing year, a chapter unfolds,
In the bittersweet journey as we grow old.

The pace may slow, the steps may falter,
Yet the spirit within never does alter.
We carry with us the joys and the tears,
The laughter, the sorrows, the hope, and the fears.

In the mirror's reflection, we see the years gone by,
A roadmap of experiences, reaching the sky.
The wrinkles and silver, symbols of time's hold,
A testament to the stories of growing old.

But in the quiet moments, a wisdom is found,

A depth of understanding, profound and round.

For in growing old, we learn to let go,

Embracing each moment, letting life flow.

embrace the journey, with hearts full and bold,

For the grace of aging, new treasures unfold.

With gratitude and acceptance, may our spirits be stilled,

As we walk the path of growing old, with hearts fulfilled.

Cancer

Cancer invades your body, breaking your soul down.
Making you a smaller version of the man you always
were.
Cancer took over your heart and made it harder to let
go.

Life will go on, but you will not be here to carry us
forward like you did for many years.
Cancer is the pain of losing you this way, never
knowing what could have been and what should have
been.

You live in our hearts and give us strength, but we'd
rather have you instead of the memories you left
behind.
Cancer is what tore us all apart and made us lose your
love that day.

Cancer is the poison within our bodies that awakens
with vengeance
and rips our hearts out of our chests,
never knowing what the future will hold for our family.

Scars

These scars tell my story.
The story of a child who survived when all odds were against
her.

I carry these scars with pride, for I overcame the
abuse that tore my skin open.
I carry these scars on my body so
I know what to never allow in my life again.

These scars are ugly,
but they are a big part of being a survivor.

These scars are a part of me and come from different parts of my
life.
They are my reminder of how hard I fight.

These scars are not only on my body, but on my heart and mind.
These scars taught me how mean people are,
but also taught me why I should love.

These scars tell my story
and how God put me back together again.

I was broken and left for dead,
but God renewed and restored who I was.

These scars I carry so I can prove to you all that happened.
I love my scars
and hope to show you what God can do.

Daily Mantra

I am a child of God!

I am loved

I am going to be alright

God loves me! And will provide.

I am Redeemed.

May these echoes remind you that silence is
not emptiness, but space for your soul to rise.
Carry what heals you, release what breaks you

And know every echo of you is enough.

Thank You!

☾ Echoes of Me: Poems of Loss and Healing

✧ Thank You

Thank you for journeying through these poems with me. *Echoes of Me* was born out of loss, but also out of resilience — the act of putting words to grief and rediscovering who I am after my mother's passing. Your support means more than I can express, and I am honored that you've chosen to spend time in these pages with me.

🌐 Stay Connected

I love building a community of readers, dreamers, and healers who believe in the power of words.

- 📱 Instagram: @author_RachelNorman — poetry readings, behind-the-scenes glimpses, and encouragement for anyone navigating grief and healing.

- 🎵 TikTok: @authorrachelnorman

- 🌐 randrnorman.com — my home base online, where you'll find updates on books, creative projects, and more.

📖 Don't Miss My Other Books

If *Echoes of Me* resonated with you, you may also love:

- 🌸 *Reflections of Her: Poems of Memory and Love* — a tender tribute to my mother's life, legacy, and the beauty of the love she left behind.

- 🙏 *I Surrender, God* — a prayer journal created to help you lay your burdens at His feet and find strength in surrender.

- 🌼 *Thankful, Grateful, Blessed* — a daily prayer journal designed to cultivate gratitude, peace, and joy in every season of life.

About the Author

Rachel Norman is a writer, poet, and storyteller whose work is rooted in faith, resilience, and the enduring power of memory. Through her words, she captures the rawness of grief, the beauty of healing, and the strength found in carrying forward the legacies of those we love.

Reflections of Her and *Echoes of Me* were born from Rachel's own journey of losing her mother and learning to navigate life, love, and motherhood without her. Her poetry reflects both the ache of absence and the hope found in remembrance, offering comfort to others who walk the path of loss.

When she's not writing, Rachel is deeply passionate about faith, family, and creating safe spaces where stories of pain can be transformed into testimonies of strength. She hopes her words will remind every reader that though loss changes us forever, love has the power to echo through generations.

Other Books by Rachel Norman

Reflection of Her

A tender collection of poems written in memory of my mother — her love, her presence, and the ways she shaped my life. These poems are the reflections of her legacy, the mirror of who she was to me, and the light she left behind.

Echoes of Me

Where Reflection of Her ends, Echoes of Me begins. This collection carries the weight of my grief and the steps I took to walk through my mother's passing. It is the sound of my healing, the echoes of my voice learning to rise again, and the poetry of survival and faith.

Together, these two books form a conversation: one looks back at the beauty of her life, while the other reveals the journey of moving forward after loss.

I Surrender, God (Yearly Prayer Journal)

A journal created for those who are ready to lay their worries and battles at the feet of God. With space for prayer, surrender, and reflection, this book serves as a guide to finding peace through letting go and trusting Him daily.

Thankful, Grateful, and Blessed (Yearly Prayer Journal)

A gentle reminder to see God's blessings in every season.
This yearly journal is filled with space to record gratitude,
prayers, and reflections — helping you stay rooted in
thankfulness, no matter what life brings.

"These works are pieces of my heart — my grief, my
healing, and my faith poured onto the page. May they meet
you in your own story and remind you that even in loss,
love and hope remain.

www.ingramcontent.com/pod-product-compliance
Lightning Source LLC
Chambersburg PA
CBHW051209120626
46547CB00013B/1276